Look What You Can Make With

Paper Plates

Edited by Margie Hayes Richmond
Photographs by Hank Schneider

Boyds Mills Press

Editorial Consultant:

Beth Murray

Craft Coordinator:

Sharon Dunn Umnik

Craftmakers:

Judy Burke
Joan O'Donnell
Kathy Murray Pietraszewski
Linda Rindock
Linda Rose
Sharon Dunn Umnik

Contributors:

Patricia Barley
Katherine Bartow
B. Beitler
Linda Bloomgren
Judy Burke
Kathy Everett
Tanya Turner Fry
Pamela Gallo
Juanita Galuska
Lory Golden

Helen Jeffries
Janet Hobbs Johnson
Tama Kain
Twilla Lamm
Beth Lehlbach
Agnes Maddy
Cheri Michels
Beth Murray
Mary Ellen Norton
Jeff O'Hare

James Perrin
Kathy Pietraszewski
Deanna Peters
Jane K. Priewe
Margie H. Richmond
Kathy Ross
Gloria Stanton
Sharon Dunn Umnik
Linda Ward
Debra K. Zimmerman

Published by Bell Books
Boyds Mills Press, Inc.
A Highlights Company
815 Church Street
Honesdale, Pennsylvania 18431
Printed in China

Publisher Cataloging-in-Publication Data
Look what you can make with paper plates / edited by Margie Hayes Richmond ; photographs by Hank Schneider.—1st ed.
[48]p. : col.ill. ; cm.
Summary : Paper plates are transformed into a vast array of toys, games, decorations, and gifts.

1. Paper work—Juvenile literature. 2. Handicraft—Juvenile literature.
[1. Paper work. 2. Handicraft.] I. Richmond, Margie Hayes. II. Schneider, Hank, ill. III. Title.
745.562—dc20   1997   AC   CIP
Library of Congress Catalog Card Number 96-85993

First edition, 1997
Book designed by Lorianne Siomades
The text of this book is set in 10pt. Avant Garde Demi, titles 43pt. Gill Sans Extra Bold

Getting Started

This book is crammed full of fun, easy-to-make crafts that each begin with a paper plate. You'll find a wide variety of things to make, including holiday decorations, gifts, toys, and games.

Directions

Read all the directions for each craft before you start. Big, beautiful photographs make following the step-by-step directions a snap. This really is a time when "a picture is worth a thousand words." The picture will help you better understand how to make the craft and will inspire you to make yours beautiful and unique. When we tell you to "decorate," that means use paint, crayons, markers, or whatever you like to make your craft colorful and personal. Let your imagination soar, but always remember that paint and glue need time to dry!

Work Area

It's always best to protect your clothing and work surface. So you may want to wear a smock or apron. A parent's or older sibling's old shirt works nicely, too. Simply trim off or roll up the sleeves. Next, cover the floor, table, or counter top where you will work with paper. Old newspapers are great. Or you can cut up large brown-paper grocery bags and tape a few together. Some craft-makers use old worn-out sheets. Remember to clean up when you're done!

Materials

Gather craft-making supplies and put them into a box or basket that you can keep handy. The picture below shows most of the basic craft-making supplies you will need. You can add other items as you think of them. You'll see that each craft in the book has a list of materials you may need. Get all those things together before you start making your craft. If you intend to make only one of the crafts pictured on a page, check the directions against the materials list. You may not need all the items listed.

Very Important

You'll find that many crafts have ideas for three or four different crafts based on one basic idea and set of directions. Plus every craft is presented with a *More Ideas* section. You'll also think of new ideas of your own once you get rolling. So browse through these pages, choose a craft, and have some creative fun. Before you know it, you'll be exclaiming, "Look what I *made* with paper plates!"

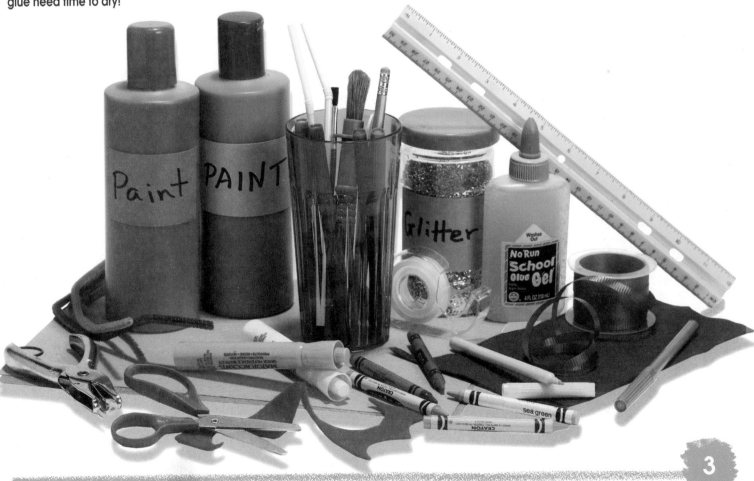

Pigs, Pugs, and Pachyderms

You can make a pen full of pigs, a cute little pet pug dog, or your own zoo full of pachyderms with these easy directions. (*Pachyderms* is a fancy name for elephants, rhinos, and hippos.)

You Will Need:

- sturdy paper plates
- flexible paper plates
- paint
- glue
- cardboard tubes
- scissors
- construction paper
- small paper cup
- chenille stick
- yarn

To Make the Basic Animal

1 Use 8-10 sturdy plates to make the body of each animal. You might want to use lunch-sized plates for the pigs and pugs and dinner-sized plates for the pachyderms. Paint the bottoms and edges of the plates. Glue 4 pairs of plates together, rim-to-rim, with the painted sides facing out. Cut out ears from a painted flexible paper plate and glue them between the remaining two plates. This will be your animal's head. Glue all the pairs of plates back-to-back.

2 Make the legs from whole or pieces of cardboard tubes. Because there is glue on the tubes, you may want to cover them with white paper and then paint to get a more even coloring. Glue the tubes to the body where the legs would be. The tubes fit between the sets of plates nicely. Glue on eyes, eyelashes, toenails, and tails made from construction paper or other materials.

So stock up on your paper plates and paint. All your friends are going to want to make a clever creation of their own.

To Make the Pug

Make the body and legs of the pug dog, following the basic directions. Then cut out ears, a nose, and a tail. Remember that a pug's ears fold down. We made our pug "sit." Instead of gluing the sets of plates in a straight row, we dropped each set down about 1" so that the row is angled. Glue the tubes horizontally for his back legs.

To Make the Pig

Make the body of the pig, following the basic directions. Add legs. Then cut out ears, a nose, and a tail, making sure they're the right size and shape. We made our pig's nose from a small paper cup. A curled-up chenille stick makes a great pig's tail. Use your imagination. How about cutting a slit in the top of your pig's back for a perfect piggy bank?

To Make the Elephant

Follow the basic directions to make the elephant. Cut ears and a trunk from flexible plates. Remember to paint all plates first. We made our elephant a realistic gray. You can make yours pink or polka-dotted. Glue all features to the head. We gave our elephant big eyes, a braided yarn tail, and a paper bow tie.

More Ideas

You can make almost any animal using this basic idea. Try covering the bodies with fabric or papier-mâché. Bulldogs, hippos, and rhinos are obvious choices. But can you make a buffalo or an armadillo? How about a giant three-dimensional centipede to "crawl" around your room?

Magnet Track

Make your own toy.

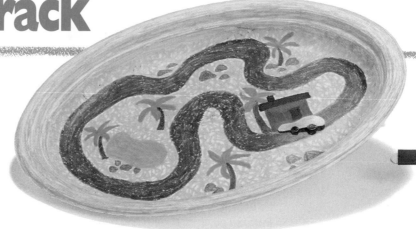

You Will Need:
- flexible paper plate
- crayons
- thin cardboard
- glue
- small magnets
- ice-cream stick

1 Draw an automobile racetrack on the plate. Make it a winding, mazelike road course. Create a scene by drawing in hills, lakes, boulders, and other obstacles. Cut out a car from thin cardboard. Decorate it and then glue it to the magnet.

2 Glue another small magnet to the ice-cream stick. (Be sure to place the two magnets so that they attract, rather than repel, each other.) Hold the stick under the plate and guide your car around the track. Hold "time trials" to improve your speed.

More Ideas

Make a racetrack for horses or create a train track. Any kind of maze will work, too. Try a rocket to the Moon or a bee to flowers. We used a sturdy platter, but the magnets work best with the thinner types of plates.

Anyone-Can-Do-It Stick Puppet

Making a stick puppet is easy. And when you're done, it's fun to play with.

You Will Need:
- paper plate
- paint, crayons, markers
- colored paper
- scissors
- yarn
- ice-cream stick
- glue

1 Decorate a paper plate to look like a face, using crayons, markers, and colored-paper cutouts. Use yarn for the hair. How about making the puppet a self-portrait?

2 Glue the ice-cream stick to the middle of the back of the plate; decorate it if you like. Have fun with your puppet.

More Ideas

Get your friends or family members to make puppets of their own. Then you can put on a play together, or pretend that your puppets are having a conversation. Your puppets might even help you settle an argument with a sibling or friend. It's hard to stay angry using your puppet voice!

Disguise Master Mask

You can be a master of disguises. Make one mask or a whole wardrobe of them from plates or platters. Which of the ones we made is your favorite?

You Will Need:

- paper plate or platter
- pencil
- scissors
- construction paper
- markers
- various items for decorations
- yarn or elastic
- stapler

1 Hold the front side of the plate against your face. Find where your eyes and mouth would be and carefully mark lightly with a pencil. It's best to get a grown-up to help you.

2 Draw eye holes and a mouth hole and cut them out. Hold the plate up to your face again to be sure the eye holes are large enough for you to see through safely.

3 Decorate the face with markers and construction-paper cutouts. You may want to cut the plate into a special shape as we did for our bear. Add details, such as chenille-stick whiskers, a button or cup nose, paper ears, or yarn hair or mane.

4 You can use yarn or elastic to tie your mask in place. If you use elastic, measure one piece that is long enough to fit comfortably over your head. Or cut two equal pieces of yarn. Staple one end of each piece of yarn or elastic to the back side rim of your mask, just below the eye level.

More Ideas

Hang your masks around your room like pictures. People can admire your artistic talent. Use smaller plates and make masks for dolls or stuffed animals. These masks make great wall decorations, too.

Invite friends over for a mask-making party and then make up a play that involves each mask as a character. Or have a Halloween party and have a mask for each of your guests.

7

Double-Ups

You can double up paper plates for double the fun. And it won't be hard to keep doubling your ideas for things to make. You might want to start with some of the "double-ups" pictured here.

You Will Need:

- sturdy paper plates and bowls
- paint, crayons, markers
- yarn or ribbon
- stapler or glue
- paper punch
- colored paper
- dry beans
- bottle cap or film container
- egg carton
- chenille stick
- foil
- tape

1 Decide how big you want your "double-up" to be and start with the right-sized plates. Bowls or platters will work, too. Paint or color the bottoms of the plates to suit your plan. It's almost always better to paint your plates as the very first step. Remember to allow time for the paint to dry.

2 Put the plates together face-to-face. You can choose to weave, staple, or glue the edges of the plates together. To weave, start by punching holes around the two plates. Space the holes evenly about 1/2" to 1" apart. Thread yarn or ribbon up and down through each hole. (Leave enough yarn or ribbon at the beginning so that you can tie it to the other end when you've finished.) Wrapping the end of the yarn with tape and twisting it will make it easier to thread through the holes. You can cut that part off when you're done.

To Make the Flying Saucer

Attach the two plates rim-to-rim as previously described. We glued ours. For the top of your spacecraft, place the bowl upside down on the doubled plates. You can make four landing-gear legs from parts of an egg carton. Let the glue dry and decorate your flying saucer. We added a sparkly chenille-stick antenna and foil windows. You could make a bigger three-tiered craft by using platter-sized plates for a bottom layer. Happy landings!

Read the directions before you begin. There are some slight variations that you need to be aware of early in the creative process.

To Make the Card Caddy

Choose and decorate your plates. We used a colored plate for our caddy's back and used paint on the front plate. Cut off the top third of one paper plate and discard. Then staple, weave, or glue that partial plate's rim to the whole plate's rim. Create a strap from ribbon or yarn. Hang your caddy on a doorknob—it's a great place for your mail, special-occasion cards, keys, and important notes.

To Make the Bean Tambourine

Follow Steps 1 and 2, but stop weaving when there are a few holes left. Pour dry beans into the space between the plates. Finish weaving and tie a knot in the yarn at the first hole. Now decorate your tambourine, and you're ready to add a rhythmic beat to your next sing-along.

To Make the Pretend Canteen

Decorate and "double up" two plates. We sponge painted ours and added strips of felt. Make a cap for your canteen out of a bottle cap or an empty film container. Cut two small slits on opposite sides of the container's rim and slide it onto the top of the canteen. We added a safety string to our cap. Add a cloth or wide ribbon strap. Or you can make a "belt loop" by cutting a piece of cloth and attaching its ends to the back of the canteen. Slip your canteen on your belt and head into the wild. Remember, it's "pretend," so it won't hold water.

More Ideas

Double up plates to make a pretend tiered layer cake for a centerpiece for a birthday party or other special celebration.

Create a clown "piggy bank." Just lay your double-up flat and decorate to look like a clown's face. Cut a slit in its mouth and drop in your pennies.

Turn your tambourine into a drum. Make a drumstick from a wooden dowel with a wadded tissue-paper knob.

Can you imagine how to turn the canteen into a turtle or the card caddy into a purse?

Ice Skater

Ice skaters are strong, graceful, flexible . . . and their costumes are always beautiful. Have fun using paper plates to design your own winning outfit.

You Will Need:

- flexible paper plates
- chenille sticks
- scissors
- glitter
- paint
- stapler

1 To form the body, place two chenille sticks vertically side-by-side. Twist them together about three quarters of the way from the top, making legs. About one quarter of the way from the top, wrap another chenille stick around to form arms.

2 To form the front and back of the skirt, fold and cut a flexible paper plate in half. Glue the plate halves together with the bottoms facing out. Cut other layers for the skirt from more paper plates, making the front of these plates face out. Cut the bodice for the front and back from a paper plate. Paint all the sections and let dry. Add glitter. Place the chenille-stick body between the dress sections and staple together.

3 From scrap paper-plate pieces, cut out a head and ice skates. Decorate and glue them to the body. Bend the arms and legs in different positions.

More Ideas

Create your own ice-skating rink by cutting and gluing several pieces of corrugated cardboard together. Cover the surface with construction paper, paint, or foil. Make several skaters with their arms and legs in different skating positions. Glue or tape a wooden skewer to the back of each skater and press the pointed end of the skewer into the ice-skating rink. Use as a centerpiece for a pre-ice-skating party or when you just invite friends over to watch ice-skating on TV.

You can follow the basic directions to make a Cinderella doll all dressed for the ball. Or try making bride and groom dolls. You and your friends might even create "models" for a pretend fashion show.

A Plate for All Seasons

Beautiful scenes are often shown on china plates. Plates can be a natural "canvas" for your great works of art.

You Will Need:

- 4 paper plates
- glue
- colored paper
- poster board
- crayons, markers
- scissors

1 Decide what scene you want to create. We've done the same outdoor scene as it would look for each season of the year. Let your imagination be your guide—you could make a plate for each of your favorite holidays. A series of fish or birds might be fun to do.

2 Decorate the edge of the plates to look like frames. (We mounted each plate on a cut-out black poster board circle.) Create your scenes with paint, crayons, or glued-on colored-paper cutouts.

More Ideas

Use black paper on white plates to do a series of silhouettes. Or how about a series of old-fashioned-looking cameos in cream and tan?

Three-Plate Wall Hanging

You can make a wall hanging for any special day. The possibilities are endless.

1 Cut three printed fabric circles slightly larger than the plates. Glue the fabric on the front of each plate, wrapping it around the edges. Cut letters or designs from solid-color felt—we did MOM on heart-print fabric. Glue one letter or design to each plate.

2 Punch holes in the rim of each plate and string them together with ribbon. Add a bow and a ribbon loop for a hanger.

More Ideas

Make Valentine's Day plates spell out I LOVE YOU. Or make Christmas plates spell out JOY or NOEL (using 4 plates).

You Will Need:

- 3 dessert-sized paper plates
- printed and solid-color fabric or felt
- glue
- ribbon or yarn

Things with Wings

Choose "something with wings" that you want to make. We made an eagle, a bat, a moth, and a butterfly—sections of paper-plate rims make great feathers.

You Will Need:

- flexible paper plates
- cardboard tubes
- construction paper, poster board
- scissors
- tape or glue
- paint, crayons, markers
- glitter
- chenille sticks

To Make the Body and Head

1 Choose the color you want your flying friend to be. We used realistic colors for our eagle and butterfly, but then we let our imaginations take flight with the bat. Wouldn't a red-white-and-blue eagle make a great centerpiece for a Fourth of July or Memorial Day picnic?

2 Get a cardboard tube for each craft you want to make. A paper towel tube is good for taller winged creatures and a bathroom tissue tube works well for smaller flyers. Cover the tube with colored construction paper or with white paper and then paint it. (We found if you paint the tube itself, the glue that holds the tube together shows through.) Just remember to leave time for the paint to dry.

3 Draw a head for your flyer on construction paper or poster board and cut it out. Glue it to the top of the tube. Add features with crayon, marker, paint, cut paper, or chenille sticks. We even used glitter. Be sure to give your winged thing its own personality—we made a fierce eagle and a friendly bat.

You can make a whole flock of flying things. How about attaching strings to hang them from the ceiling or from a painted cardboard ring for a "winged-thing" mobile?

To Make the Eagle

Cut wings from construction paper or poster board. We used two layers to give our eagle a majestic wingspan. To create "feathers" for the wings, use the ripply rims of paper plates. The ripples will add texture and dimension. First color or paint the rims. (We used black, brown, and yellow and colored with a feathery stroke.) Next, cut the colored rims into small sections and glue them on the wings. Glue the wings to the tube body, add eagle feet, and your toy is ready to fly.

To Make the Bat

Cut wings from poster board or construction paper. Color the ripply rim of a paper plate or use a colored plate like we did. Cut the rim into small pieces. Glue the pieces onto the wings. (We used black wings with purple cutouts.) Attach the bat wings to its body, and you've got a great Halloween friend.

To Make the Butterfly

Cut wing shapes from paper plates and decorate. Use the ripply rims for the outer edges of the wings or cut the rims apart to decorate the insect's body. Add antennae and legs made from chenille sticks or pieces of paper plate and glue in place. Attach the wings to the tubes. We liked this idea so much we made a glittery moth, too. Our butterfly's body is horizontal, and the moth is flying upright. Why not brighten someone's day by giving them one of these colorful creations?

More Ideas

You can make a different kind of head for your creature. A small paper cup turned upside down on top of the tube works really well, especially for larger birds, such as eagles or hawks.

Think of all kinds of things with wings. How about a flock of geese or ducks? Their natural coloration is beautiful. Can you make an elegant swan or turn a long wrapping-paper tube into a stand-up angel with paper-plate wings?

Spinning Mix-Ups

Here's a game that makes "making faces" fun. It's easy.

You Will Need:

- 2 dinner-sized paper plates
- 1 dessert-sized paper plate
- pencil
- ruler
- metal fastener
- markers or crayons

1 Mark the centers of all three plates. Cut off the rims of the small and one large plate. Join all three at the center with a metal fastener, putting the smallest plate on top and the largest on the bottom. Draw straight lines through the connected plates so it looks like a pie with four even slices.

2 In each of the four sections, draw a pair of eyes on the top layer, a nose in the middle layer, and a mouth on the bottom. Spin your wheel! See the many different faces you can make.

More Ideas

Buildings, monsters, flowers, even ice-cream sundaes can be fun to mix and spin, too.

Small-Present Package

Make a "package" in which to present a special present.

You Will Need:

- paper bowl
- sturdy paper plate
- pencil
- hole punch
- yarn
- crayons, markers
- felt
- scissors

1 Decorate the bottom of the bowl. Put it in the center of the plate and lightly trace its outline. Ask an adult to help you poke holes 1/4" within the circle you drew. Decorate inside the circle and the rest of the plate.

2 Punch holes (spaced the same as those in the plate) around the edge of the bowl. Use yarn to weave the bowl and plate together face-to-face. Now you can open and close the package.

More Ideas

Hang your package on the wall and you've got a secret safe. Or add a strap to make a purse.

The Great Plate Caper Game

You can use paper plates to make a great game to play with your friends. So gather some together and have lots of fun.

You Will Need:

- sturdy dessert-sized paper plate
- paper cup
- sturdy dinner-sized paper plates (with a "lip" rim)
- scissors
- paint, crayons, markers
- tape or glue
- construction paper
- large paper clip
- metal fastener
- assorted buttons

To Make the Game Board

1 Use the bottom of the dessert-sized plate and draw squares around the border. Number each square in order from 1 to 16. This will be the dial of the game board.

2 To make the handle of the dial, cut off and discard the top half of the paper cup. Then cut several 1/2" slits around the top. Decorate and press the cup upside down against the plate, fanning out the slitted flaps. Tape or glue the flaps to the plate.

3 Paint one of the dinner-sized plates a different color or use a colored paper plate. Set the "dial plate" inside this plate. Draw an arrow on the edge of the larger plate or cut one from paper and glue it on. This will be the game board pointer.

To Make the Spinner

1 Decorate the bottom of a dinner-sized plate. Draw two lines so they divide the bottom into four equal sections (pizza style). Number the sections 1 through 4. Make a hole in the center of the plate.

2 You can use a large paper clip for a spinner. Attach it to the plate with a metal fastener. Make sure the fastener is a little loose so the paper clip will spin.

More Ideas

You can make all kinds of spinners to use in other games. Make more than 4 sections and mark them with a variety of colors, letters, or symbols.

How to Play the Game

Each player places a button on or above one of the numbered sections of the game board.

Players take turns thumping the paper-clip spinner. The number where it stops tells them how many spaces they can turn the dial on the game board. Players can move in either direction, but in only one direction per turn.

The object is to get the button to the game board pointer. The first button to reach the pointer wins.

Paper-Plate Party

You can plan a whole party around paper plates—from creating your own decorations to inventing games and activities. Choose a color scheme or theme for your party and decorate accordingly.

You Will Need:

- a variety of paper plates
- scissors
- paint, crayons, markers, watercolors
- stapler, tape, or glue
- sponge
- straws
- ribbon
- waxed paper
- rubber band

To Make a Party Hat

1 To make the hat brim, draw a circle 1 1/2" in from the edge of a paper plate.

2 Draw your design in the center of the plate, with the bottom of the design touching the circle. We drew a western hat shape.

3 Color or paint your design, then cut away the background area between it and the circle, leaving the bottom of your design attached to the brim. Bend the design part of the hat forward. Add a guest's name.

To Make Goody Boxes

1 Paint both sides of a paper plate. Fold it in half, crease, then unfold. Do the same thing the other way; the creases divide the plate into equal sections.

2 Fold two opposite sides of the paper plate into the center. (The edges should just touch with no overlap.) Crease, then unfold. Do the same thing the other way. This will make a square, which will be the bottom of the box.

3 Beyond each corner of the square is a small rounded triangle. Pull each triangle out, fold down the center, and staple. Do the same thing to all four corners. Decorate the box and fill it with favors or treats.

To Make a Horn

1 Color or paint a flexible dinner-sized plate. Cut one edge off to form a straight side about 6" long. Then roll the paper plate to form a cone. Tape or glue to hold in place. You may still need to trim the straight side evenly for the end. Decorate your horn.

2 Cut a 4" circle of waxed paper and place it over the large end of the cone. Hold in place with a rubber band. We taped a piece of ribbon over the rubber band. Then hum into the other end of the horn and make your own party music.

To Make Personalized Place Cards

1 Fold a small paper plate in half and then open it. Cut out a shape on the top half of the plate. We made a face wearing a western hat. Your shape can be anything that suits your own party theme.

2 Decorate. To sponge paint like we did all our party crafts, just dip a small section of sponge in some watercolor and dab on the plates. When dry, write on a guest's name.

Have a pre-party craft-making get-together. Just gather your paper plates and other crafting materials and invite a couple of friends over a few days before the party date.

To Make a Centerpiece

1 To make the holder part of the centerpiece, color or paint the bottom of a sturdy dinner-sized paper plate. Cut it in half and attach the two halves rim-to-rim with glue or staples.

2 To make a base for your centerpiece, decorate the bottom of a sturdy plate and cut a 4" slit in its center. Slide the bottom of the holder part into the slit. Pour a little glue into the slit if you need more support to make the centerpiece stand up straight.

3 Decide what you want to feature in your centerpiece. To make balloons like ours, cut out and decorate paper balloon shapes. Cut a small slit near the top and bottom of each balloon. Add a guest's name. Insert a straw in the slits and place it in the centerpiece. Everyone can take a straw when the refreshments are served.

More Ideas

Make a card caddy like the one shown on page 8. Just decorate it to fit your party theme and hang it where guests can put in their cards.

Make color-coordinated streamers to hang from the ceiling. Just follow the directions found on page 24.

Make and play the paper-plate games described on pages 14, 15, and 36. Again, you may want to decorate your plates to match your other creations.

Plate Playmates

Hand puppets are great playmates. You can use paper plates to make one or a bunch. And you can make them as playful pals or merry monsters.

You Will Need:

- flexible dinner-sized paper plate
- paint, crayons, markers
- pencil
- bathroom tissue tube
- scissors
- construction and heavy paper
- glue
- tape

1 Fold a flexible paper plate in half and then open it. The bottom of the plate will be your puppet's outer section. Paint or color it. Paint or color the front area of the plate the way you want the inside of the puppet's mouth to look.

2 You can make eyes for your playmate. Just hold the tube upright on a sheet of white paper and trace around its bottom twice. Add a tab to each of the circles you drew and cut them out. Decorate.

3 Cover the cardboard tube with construction paper and cut it in half. Glue the two tubes side-by-side to the top outside half of the plate. These will be your puppet's eye sockets. Glue the tabs of the eyes you made in Step 2 to the inside of the tubes.

4 When completely dry, add features. One of our puppets has paper teeth, tongue, and long eyelashes. And don't you love our frog's dinner? Have fun thinking up cool things for your own playmate.

5 Cut a 3"- by -1" strip of heavy paper, form it into a loop, and tape it securely to the outside of the bottom half of the plate. Be sure your thumb can fit into the loop. Slip your thumb into the paper loop and your index and middle fingers into the back of the eyes and make your puppet come to life.

More Ideas

You can give your playmates hair made from yarn, curly ribbon, or even curly construction paper. To make curly paper strips, just wind them around a pencil and hold for a while. Then unwind.

Make a bull or unicorn; just add horns to your puppet. Add paper flames for a fierce-but-friendly fire-breathing dragon.

Decorate your plate to look like a clam or even a crab. Or how about an oyster shell with a pearl inside?

Invite friends over for a Plate-Playmate-Making Party and then create a play to perform for friends and family.

Angel Chorus

Many people collect angels. Do you?

You Will Need:

- dessert-sized flexible plates
- glue, stapler, or tape
- scissors
- paint, crayons, markers
- chenille sticks
- glitter

1 Cut a plate in half. Curve the half-plate into a cone. Staple, glue, or tape in place. Cut wings from paper-plate rims. Decorate the body and wings.

2 Create a face, hands, and songbook; glue them and the wings to the body. Tape a chenille-stick halo to the back of the angel's head.

More Ideas

Create a glee club. Just leave off the wings and halos and paint the bodies to look like choir robes.

Yarn Art Star

Create a hanging Star of David.

You Will Need:

- flexible dinner-sized paper plate
- yarn
- crayons
- tape
- scissors or hole punch

1 Punch 6 evenly spaced holes about 1" from the outside edge of the plate. Cut 6 slits about 3" in toward the center. Put slits halfway between holes.

2 To make the small star you'll connect the slits. Begin by taping one end of a long piece of yarn to the back of the plate. String the yarn through a slit and across the plate to the next slit. When the star is complete, tape the back of the slits.

3 You'll connect the holes to form the large Star of David. Finish by taping the other end of the yarn to the plate's back and make a hanger.

More Ideas

Try to make geometric shapes with 5, 6, 8, 10, or 12 sides.

Rockin' Crafts

Get ready to rock 'n' roll with a variety of fun things to make. The base of each one is a rocker. And would you believe that each rocker is made from a paper plate?

You Will Need:

- flexible paper plates
- ruler
- pencil
- paint, crayons, markers
- construction paper
- scissors
- small tissue box
- felt, fabric
- drinking straws
- glue
- yarn or chenille sticks
- thin cardboard

To Make the Rocker

1 Lightly fold a plate in half and then unfold it. Using a ruler, draw two straight lines 1 1/2" on either side of the fold. For a broader top area on the rocker, draw your lines farther apart.

2 Fold the paper plate along each of the lines you drew. (Make sure the folds are straight so your craft will rock straight.) Color or paint the rocker.

3 If your craft seems a little head or tail heavy, use a coin or paper clip to balance it. Just tape the "weight" underneath the bottom of the rocker's flat part. This trick will also work if you want your rockin' craft to tip one way more than the other.

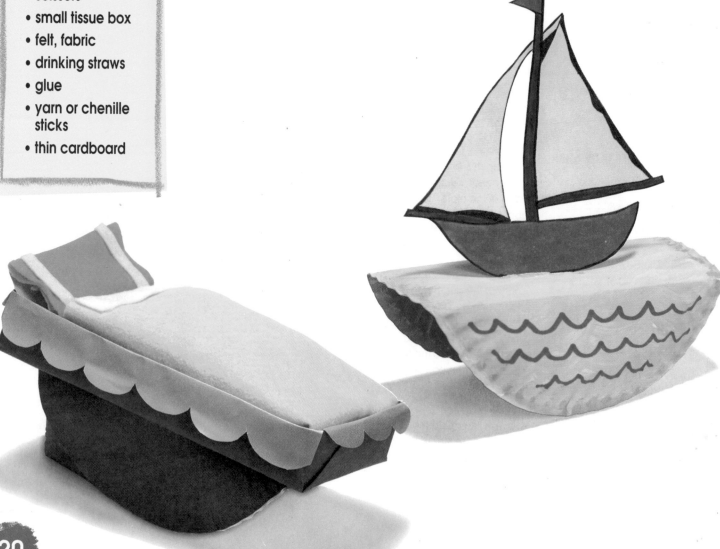

We've made four very different rockin' creations that will make great gifts, especially for your younger friends or family members.

To Make the Rockin' Cradle

Make and decorate the rocker as described in Steps 1 and 2. We painted our rocker brown and decorated it with yellow scallops cut from paper. To make the bed part, cut the bottom 2" off an empty tissue box and glue felt or other material to its inside bottom. (The cotton that comes in the box when you buy jewelry would make a great soft mattress.) Glue completed bed onto the flat portion of the rocker. You might want to make a blanket and pillow for your cradle from scraps of fabric. You could also make a canopy. Use cut-up drinking straws for bedposts and felt or lacy fabric for the canopy top.

To Make the Rockin' Horse

Follow Steps 1 and 2 to create the rocker. Then make a 1" slit about 1/2" in from the front edge of the rocker top. You will use this slit to insert the head. Make the horse's head from a paper plate or cardboard. Color the head with paint, markers, or crayons. Use yarn, felt, or construction paper to form the features. Make a horse tail by gluing or taping a bundle of cut yarn or twist and bend a bundle of chenille sticks. A combination of yarn and chenille sticks works well, too. Poke a hole toward the back of the rocker top. Make it just large enough to fit in the tail.

To Make the Rockin' Boat

Follow Steps 1 and 2. Paint or color water on the rocker. Create a colorful boat with cut-out colored paper, paint, or markers. We drew a sailboat on cardboard, colored it with markers, and cut it out. Remember to make tabs at the bottom of the boat. Cut a 2" to 3" slit in the center of the top of the rocker and insert the boat's tabs. Bend the ends of tabs and tape them underneath to keep the boat on the "water."

More Ideas

You can make rockin' ducks, turkeys, or just about any one of your favorite animals. Look at the brightly colored parrot we made using a blue paper plate for the rocker.

Try your hand at making a rocking chair. Just make a ladder-style back and arms from heavy paper or thin cardboard.

Cup 'n Platter Warehouse

Here's a pretty storage warehouse for small treasures.

You Will Need:
- sturdy paper platter
- cardboard egg carton
- scissors
- paint, crayons, markers
- ribbon, lace
- glue

1 Paint or color the platter. Cut several cup sections from a cardboard egg carton. Color or paint. Let dry. Decorate the rim of the platter. We glued on lace.

2 Arrange the cup sections on the platter and carefully glue in place. Create a hanger and fill the cups with earrings or other small jewelry items.

More Ideas

Make a workshop organizer for nuts, bolts, and screws or even fishing tackle. Not enough cups? String two or more organizers together.

In Like a Lion, Out Like a Lamb

Make a March weather indicator.

You Will Need:
- paper plates
- paint, crayons, markers
- cotton balls
- construction paper
- scissors
- yarn
- glue
- plastic eyes
- chenille sticks

1 For the lamb, decorate the plate and glue cotton balls around its rim. Create ears, eyes, a nose, and a mouth.

2 For the lion, decorate the other plate. To make the mane, glue loops of brown yarn around the top half of the plate. Create facial features. Make whiskers from chenille sticks.

3 Glue the faces back-to-back.

More Ideas

Make a happy face and a sad face. Hang the plate on your door to let people know how you are feeling. Or make a sunshine/raincloud plate.

A Myriad of Mobiles

You can make lots of mobiles. *Lots of*—that's what *myriad* means. Your mobile can be anything. Just choose something you really like or something someone would like as a gift.

1 To make the crescent-shaped mobile, cut shapes from two sturdy paper plates and paint them. (We made a moon.) Let dry and staple or glue the two pieces together. Punch holes along the inside curve. Punch a hole at the top of the crescent and use ribbon or yarn for a hanger.

2 To make the top part of the full-plate mobile, poke two holes side-by-side and about 1/2" apart in the middle of a plate. Thread yarn through the holes and tie to form a loop. Punch four evenly spaced holes around the edge of the plate. If your mobile does not hang straight, glue a penny to the underside to help balance it.

3 Create the hanging parts of your mobile. For some hanging parts, you'll need to punch a hole at its top and insert a piece of yarn to tie to the mobile top. For types like the ghost, you can tie the yarn directly from the hanging part to the mobile top.

To Make Flowers

Create flower and leaf shapes. Remember you can see both sides, so be sure to decorate fronts and backs.

To Make Ghosts

Put a cotton ball in the middle of a napkin and pull it smoothly around the ball. Tie a long ribbon around the "neck." Glue on eyes. Make pumpkins the same way, trimming off the excess. Then cut out and attach bat shapes.

More Ideas

Make a nighttime mobile by cutting out star shapes in different sizes and covering them with aluminum foil and glitter. Or make trains or boats to hang from your mobile.

Sparkling Spirals

You'll find this so easy to do, you'll want to make spirals by the dozens. You can turn spirals into imaginary snakes, spinners to play with, or streamers to decorate for a party.

You Will Need:

- flexible paper plates
- pencil
- scissors
- glitter
- string or yarn
- watercolors, paint, markers
- old newspaper
- colored paper

To Make the Basic Spiral

1 Decide what you want your spiral to be and how many you want to make. Choose your colors and plan the design. Then gather your paper plates and have fun decorating them. Remember to do both sides.

2 With a pencil, lightly draw circular lines on the front of each plate. Make the lines about 1" apart. You can alter the width and length of your spiral by drawing your lines closer together or farther apart.

3 Cut the plate into a spiral by starting at the rim and cutting around and around, following your pencil lines. Punch a hole at what was the center of the paper plate. This will now be the top of your spiral.

To Make a Spinner

To decorate a spinner like the one we show, place two 6" paper plates on old newspaper. With watercolors and a brush, spatter paint on both sides of the plates, letting each side dry first. Of course, you can decorate yours any way you like, using paint, markers, or crayons. A touch of glitter will add sparkle. After you've decorated each plate, cut it into a spiral as described above. Tie a piece of string or yarn through the holes and hang your double spinner where you can watch it blow in the breeze. Or give your spinner even more bounce by hanging it on a piece of elastic instead of string and use it like a yo-yo or spring-type toy.

To Make a Snake

Make your basic spiral and add stripes and eyes. Then glue on fangs and a tongue cut from colored paper. You can make different kinds of realistic snakes. You'll be surprised at what beautiful colors nature gives them. You can also have fun making up totally imaginary snakes as we did. How about a flower-covered one? You'll think of lots of fun and games for your snake. Try wrapping it around your arm like a circus performer or dangling it from a tree branch or vine.

To Make Streamers

Cut very narrow spirals from the colored paper plates. Decorate the spirals with bright colors, glitter, or stickers. (The best way to add glitter is to cover the outside bottom of a *whole* colored paper plate with a glue-and-water mixture. Sprinkle on glitter, let dry, and then cut it into a streamer.) You might make your streamers even more festive by draping or attaching extra ribbon or yarn. Create yarn hangers. You could even add a tassel at the bottom of the yarn. Now you're ready to decorate a room for a party with your colorful streamers—just add a balloon or two.

More Ideas

Make a wind sock. Cut a 6"-by-12" strip from poster board. Roll it into a cylinder that is 6" long and staple the sides together. Attach 6 or 8 decorated spirals. Add yarn or ribbon to the top of the cylinder and hang your "sock" outside where it won't get wet.

Bountiful Baskets

Make a simple basket to fill with goodies or to use as a decoration. We made one for our favorite gardener and one to celebrate Valentine's Day.

You Will Need:

- dinner-sized flexible paper plate
- paint, crayons, markers
- paintbrush
- tissue paper in various colors
- paper doilies
- construction paper
- scissors
- glue
- stapler
- ribbon

1 Use a thick brush and dab paint on the back side of a paper plate or color with crayons. Let dry, then cut the plate in half. Staple or glue the two halves together face-to-face, forming a pocket.

2 Decorate your basket. Follow our directions at right or create your own design. Then punch a hole at each end of the pocket and tie a ribbon through the holes for a hanger.

To Make the Gardener's Basket

To make flowers like ours, cut small squares of tissue paper in a variety of colors. Fold each square in half and then in half again. Hold by the folded corner and twist a few times. Fluff out the loose corners and glue the twisted part to the side of the plate. Cut out and glue on leaves. Fill the basket with packets of flower seeds, cards, gifts, or other treats.

To Make the Valentine Basket

To make our Valentine's Day basket, cut sections from paper doilies and glue to the front of the basket. Add paper hearts on top along with more pieces of paper doily.

More Ideas

Instead of flowers, make tissue-paper fish—just twist so that you form body and tail sections. Fill with small fishing items.

For even more festive baskets, punch several holes at the bottom and tie ribbon bows or streamers in each hole.

Face Plates

You can make lots of faces from plates.

You Will Need:

- dinner-sized flexible paper plate
- scissors
- paint, crayons
- construction paper
- yarn
- glue

1 Cut off about 2/3 of the rim of a paper plate, leaving part of the rim as the Pilgrim's collar and the plate's center part as the face. Paint or color.

2 Using the leftover rim, cut out eyebrows, a mustache, and hair. Paint. Cut a hat and eyes from construction paper. Glue on all cutout pieces. Tape on a yarn loop for a hanger.

More Ideas

Make a Santa. Layering pieces of plate rims will make a great beard. Can you figure out how to make a circus clown or a court jester?

Candle Light

You can make a beautiful holiday wall hanging.

You Will Need:

- platter-sized paper plate
- paint, crayons, markers
- construction paper
- scissors
- tape or glue

1 Create a menorah with candles. Above each candle, except the center one, carefully cut two curved slits to look like the sides of a flame. Make an orange paper "flame" for the center candle.

2 Cut a strip of white paper, about 1" wide and 24" long. Color half of it orange. Thread the strip through the slits. Tape its ends to form a loop.

3 Begin with the white part of the strip showing through the flame shapes. Each day of Hanukkah "light" one more candle by moving the strip.

More Ideas

Draw other holders and change the candles for other holidays.

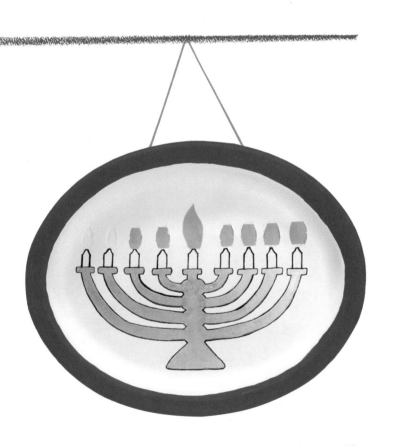

Ballerinas and Ball Games

What do ballerinas and ball games have in common? A "dome" made from a paper plate. Oh yes, you can also make a bumbershoot—that's an old-fashioned word for umbrella, you know.

You Will Need:

- flexible dinner-sized paper plates
- pencil
- scissors
- stapler
- paint, crayons, markers
- glue
- plastic straw
- metal fastener
- chenille sticks
- glitter
- small paper cup
- plastic-foam ball
- yarn
- cardboard tube

To Make the Basic Dome

1 Put the plate face up and draw a 2" circle in the center. Lightly folding the plate into 4 equal sections will help you find the center. Tracing around a small cup or other circular-shaped object is the easiest way to draw a cirlcle.

2 Cut from the edge of the plate toward the center, stopping when you get to the outside of the circle you just drew. Make another cut, in the same way, about 1/8" from the first cut. After you stop at the edge of the circle, cut back to your first line. Throw away the tiny cutout piece.

3 Repeat this procedure so that when you have completed this step the plate has 4 equal sections with a circle in the center. Overlap the sections and staple the edges. You should have a dome shape with 4 thin triangular slits.

Choose the dome craft you want to make and plan ahead. This is one of those times when you may want to decorate the plate before you make it into a dome.

To Make the Bumbershoot

Decorate your plate. If you paint it, let it dry thoroughly. Use the plate to make your dome as described in Steps 1-3. Then take a straw and make two folds, one about 1 1/4" and the other about 2 1/2" from the top of the straw. Staple the end of the straw to the straight part of the straw. You will have made a triangle with three sides that are about 1 1/4" each. Then make a hole in the middle of the top side of the triangle. Poke a metal fastener through the top center of the dome. Insert the fastener into the straw by pulling and securing the prongs through the hole you made in the straw. Cover the straw by wrapping chenille sticks around it. Insert one chenille stick inside the straw to give it stability and to form a handle. Now give your umbrella a spin!

To Make the Ballerina

The dome will be the ballerina's skirt. Design your own skirt pattern on a plate. We painted ours pink and decorated it with glitter. Make the dome. Then poke a metal fastener through its top center. Bend a straw in half, crease it, then open it. Poke a hole on the straw's crease. Attach the straw to the fastener. Bend down the two parts of the straw and you have legs. For the upper part of the body, decorate a small paper cup. Glue or tape the cup, bottom up, to the top of the skirt. Use a plastic-foam ball to form the head and use yarn for hair. Add some facial features. Attach chenille sticks or paper cutouts for arms and feet. Your ballerina is ready to twirl.

To Make the Toss-n-Scoop Ball Game

Begin by decorating a plate, a small paper cup, and a cardboard tube with paint or markers. When dry, make your dome and glue or tape the bottom of the cup to its top center. After the cup is secure, tape the tube into the base of the cup. Now just turn it over and your scoop is ready for action! Using a foam or yarn ball, toss the ball into the air and catch it in your scoop.

More Ideas

Have a friend make a scoop and play "toss and scoop" together like a game of catch.

Turn your dome upside down to make a candy dish. Creating a base from modeling clay will help it "sit" better. Protect table surfaces by putting a piece of foil on the bottom of the clay.

Decorate your dome to look like an igloo, a greenhouse, or an indoor arena for racquet sports.

Crawling Critters

It's so easy to make your favorite "bug."

You Will Need:

- paper plates
- yarn or chenille sticks
- paint, crayons, markers
- construction and waxed paper or poster board
- buttons, beads, or plastic eyes
- glue
- scissors

1 Choose the size plate that best suits the critter you want to make. With markers, crayons, or paint, color the front of the plate as your critter's body. Or if you want your critter to have a more rounded body, paint the bottom of the plate.

2 Add a head, legs, and other features with paint, markers, paper cutouts, or chenille sticks. We used small pieces of yarn dipped in glue to add fuzz to our spider and waxed paper for our bee's wings. Add button, bead, or movable plastic eyes.

More Ideas

Can you make a trudging turtle or a rollicking robot from a paper bowl? Or create a totally imaginary critter of your own.

Make several bugs to hang on your wall. Mix them with the flowers from page 47 to make a nature mural.

Everything-in-Its-Place Plates

Make a holder to keep supplies handy.

You Will Need:

- sturdy dinner-sized paper plates
- sturdy lunch-sized paper plate
- paint, crayons, markers
- glue

1 Paint the plates. Cut one plate in half and glue the two sections rim-to-rim, forming a pocket. Do the same with the other plates. Attach the pockets together, back-to-back, making a row that will stand by itself.

2 Decorate the pockets. We gave ours a funny face, but you could add rickrack, lace, or a shoestring around the edges.

More Ideas

Create a watermelon design. Fill with plates, napkins, and plastic utensils. You'll have everything in its place to take on a picnic.

Year-Round Wreath

People love to decorate with wreaths. You see them for all seasons and special occasions. Using a round paper plate is an easy way to begin your own wreath-making.

You Will Need:

- dinner-sized paper plate
- scissors
- construction paper
- glue
- various other materials (nuts, aluminum foil, stickers, glitter, seeds, ribbon, scraps of fabric, cardboard)

1 Cut out the center of the paper plate, leaving a 2" rim. Your circle doesn't have to be perfect because it is the base of the wreath and will be covered up with other materials.

2 Cut out appropriate shapes for the wreath you've chosen to make. Give your wreath extra dimension by covering shapes with foil or fabric and layering them. Add even more pizzazz with ribbons or glitter. Glue the shapes to the paper-plate circle, covering it completely.

3 Poke a hole or two in the top of the paper circle and tie on a piece of ribbon for a hanger. Adjust the length according to where you intend to place the wreath.

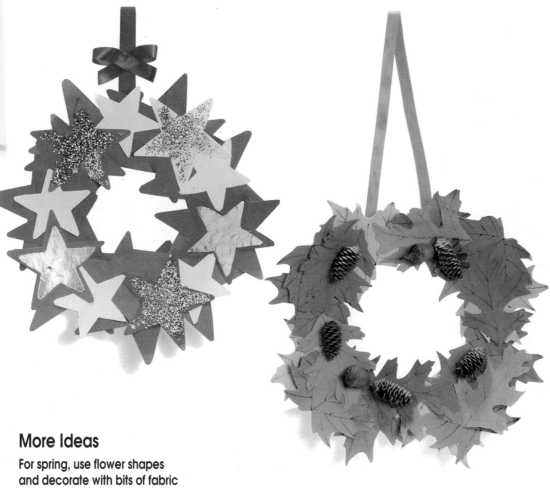

A 4th of July Wreath

Cut out star shapes from red, white, and blue construction paper and aluminum foil. Glue the star shapes around the paper plate rim, overlapping them as you go. You may want to decorate with stickers or drawings of patriotic symbols, such as flags, eagles, Uncle Sam, and the Liberty Bell.

An Autumn Wreath

Cut out leaf shapes from red, yellow, orange, and brown construction paper. You can also use leaves that you have pressed; carefully glue them onto the paper plate rim. Decorate with seeds, nuts, or different types of pinecones.

More Ideas

For spring, use flower shapes and decorate with bits of fabric or lace.

For Christmas, use holly-leaf shapes and decorate with red "berries" made from old beads or cut paper.

All in a Row

You can put paper plates "all in a row" to make a caterpillar, a dragon, and even a giraffe. Aren't the ones we made cute? They make great bedroom wall decorations.

You Will Need:

- a variety of paper plates
- paint
- yarn, ribbon, felt
- chenille sticks
- hole punch
- scissors
- construction paper
- poster board
- plastic-foam balls
- thin cardboard

To Make the Body

1 Think about how long you want the body of your creature to be. Then choose the right number and size of plates—perhaps 6 or 8 for the caterpillar, 4 for the giraffe, and 5 for the dragon. We used a variety of sizes and types. We used some colored plates and some that we painted. You can color yours with markers, crayons, or paint. Just remember to let the paint dry.

2 Using a hole punch, make holes in the rims of the plates. Punch only one hole in the plate that will be the head and one hole in the tail plate.

3 Join the plates with yarn, ribbon, or pieces of chenille stick. Arrange your animal's body and attach it to your wall or floor. Or maybe you'll want to make it a character in a play and make it "move" around like a puppet.

Silly snakes and creepy centipedes could be lots of fun to make, too. Or let your own imagination "lead you along" to create an original creature.

To Make the Dragon

Make the body as previously described. Then cut out the head and legs from thin cardboard and glue them in place. To make spikes, cut different-sized triangles from construction paper and glue them along the body, neck, and tail. Smaller spikes can be used for teeth. Add facial features with marker, paint, or glued-on paper cutouts. We made ours a friendly fire-breathing dragon. The "fire" is cutout yellow, gold, and red paper.

To Make the Giraffe

Make the head, neck, and body. Cut a tail and legs from thin cardboard. (You may want to sketch the shapes and then cut them out to be more precise.) Next draw and cut out ears, nose, and horns. Tie or tape a bundle of cut yarn and glue it to the end of the tail. Glue the tail to the body. For a realistic giraffe, use yellow paint with spots made of brown paper or fabric cutouts. Finish by making the eyes, nostrils, and mouth. Punch holes and tie on yarn for a mane.

To Make the Caterpillar

Make the body. Remember, you can make your caterpillar long or short. Use chenille sticks to make antennae. Cut pieces of felt or poster board for legs and eyebrows. Use a small plastic-foam ball cut in half for "bug" eyes.

More Ideas

You can make an alphabet row or number line to decorate a preschooler's room. Decorate each letter or number appropriately—such as an apple on the *A* plate or three little pigs on the *3* plate. In fact, your younger siblings and friends might enjoy helping you make it.

Make a name plate to put above your door. Just put the letters of your name all in a row—one per plate.

Marching Marionette

Creating your own marionette is just the beginning of the fun. Dreaming up adventures for him or her can take you all over the world.

You Will Need:

- paper plate
- scissors
- crayons or markers
- construction paper
- cardboard
- plastic straws
- heavy string

1 Decide what you want your marionette to be. Ours is a sun. Begin with a paper plate—any size will do. You may want to trim the outer edge of the plate to suit your design. We made "rays." You could create hair or a ruffly collar.

2 Draw a face on the plate or create features from yarn, paper cutouts, chenille sticks, cotton balls, or even powder puffs (for big, bushy eyebrows or a mustache).

3 Draw and cut out hands and feet from thin cardboard or construction paper. Punch holes as shown in our picture. Cut a 12"-by-1" strip from heavy cardboard for the guide bar and punch holes in it.

4 Make two pairs of tiny holes in the bottom edge of the plate for attaching legs and two more pairs where the arms will go. Put another pair of holes in the top center of the head. You'll need 5 pairs or 10 holes in all.

5 Cut drinking straws into 2" pieces. Using heavy string or twine, string 3 straw pieces together to form each leg. Tie on feet and attach the legs to the bottom of the plate. String 2 straw pieces together, attach hands, and tie arms to the plate.

6 Attach a 10" string to the ends of each hand and a 5" string to the top of the plate. Tie the arm strings to the ends of the guide bar and the head string to its center. Now you're ready to walk your marionette right through an adventure.

More Ideas

Make a moon and a star to go along with this sun.

Try making some animal marionettes. Wouldn't a monkey be fun? Or how about a wiggly octopus? But watch out for all those arms!

Get some friends to each make a wooden soldier. Then work together to see if you can get them to march in step.

Glimmering "Glass" Garden

You can make your own "stained-glass" decoration.

You Will Need:

- 2 dinner-sized flexible paper plates
- pencil
- scissors
- several colors of tissue paper
- white tissue paper
- glue
- ribbon, rickrack

1 With a pencil, lightly sketch flowers with stems on the front of one paper plate. Carefully cut out the "insides" of the flowers and stems. On the front side of the plate, glue pieces of colored tissue paper over the cutouts.

2 Cut out a 5" circle from the middle of the other plate. Cover the hole with white tissue paper glued to the plate's front.

3 Glue the plates rim-to-rim. Decorate. Attach a hanger and place near a window.

More Ideas

Your picture could be anything— try a lighthouse or an abstract geometric design.

Photo Frames

You can frame your own collage of photographs.

You Will Need:

- sturdy paper plate or platter
- photographs
- scissors
- glue or tape
- hole punch
- yarn or ribbon
- objects to trace around

1 Choose photographs, picking some that can be featured in openings of different sizes and shapes.

2 On the plate, lightly trace around small objects, such as a glass for a circle or a cassette tape holder for a rectangle. Cut out the "inside" of each shape. Decorate your frame and tape your photographs in place. (Make sure the pictures show through the openings.) Create a hanger and display your handiwork.

More Ideas

Make a family tree. Or make a blank frame and give it to new parents to use for baby pictures.

Olympic Party Time

You can use paper plates as part of a great Olympic theme party. You can make the Olympic symbol and your own medals. And you can create some Olympics-style games of your own.

You Will Need:

- sturdy dinner-sized paper plates
- flexible dessert-sized plates
- paint, crayons, markers
- scissors
- tape
- ribbon
- glue
- glitter
- coins

To Make the Olympic Symbol

1 For the symbol, cut out the insides of 5 dinner-sized sturdy plates. Put the insides aside and use later for the Number Toss. Paint or color the rings—one each of red, green, blue, gold, and black. Or use paper plates of different colors. If you want these Olympics to be distinctly your own, choose whatever colors you'd like.

2 Make one neat cut in each rim so you can interlock them, as shown on page 37. Then tape the rings back together. Hang your symbol in a prominent spot. It might be fun to make several and hang them throughout the party area.

To Make Olympic Medals

1 Paint small paper plates gold, silver, and bronze. Put glue in the shape of a star and sprinkle on glitter.

2 Tape ribbons on the back of the medals. We used gold paint on the ribbons' edges. You'll probably want to have more than one set of medals. Use them as decorations until you're ready for the medal ceremony.

Olympic Games

THE DISCUS THROW

Begin this event by creating your own Frisbee-like discus from two sturdy paper plates. Color their bottoms and glue or staple them together. Then go outdoors and let the competition begin. The discus that is thrown the greatest distance wins. Consider giving medals for improvement and funny happenings, too.

NUMBER TOSS

Use the leftover insides of the five symbol plates. Decorate and write a different number on each one. Arrange the plates on the floor. Each player has three coins, stands back about 10', and takes a turn tossing the coins. The object is to make the coins land on the "plates." The person who gets the greatest total wins.

More Ideas

AN OLYMPIC PARTY

Decorate the party area with the Olympic symbol and medals. And you can also use the ideas on pages 16 and 17 to decorate.

Serve a cake decorated with Olympic symbols surrounded by your paper-plate medals. Or make the pretend cake described on page 9 and serve Olympic-sized cookies.

Cut rectangles from the center of paper plates to make flags of a variety of countries. Sing "The Star-Spangled Banner" or play the national anthems of other nations. Did you know that some computer software will play these songs? Or let each guest create his or her own personal flag. Take turns telling what each flag symbolizes.

Nesting Plate

Here's a bright "welcome spring" centerpiece.

You Will Need:

- dessert-sized sturdy paper plate
- shredded paper or other nest-building items (twigs, sticks, string)
- glue
- tissue paper

1 Gather some nest-building materials: shredded lightweight paper, some artificial grass, or moss from an old floral or plant arrangement, for example.

2 Cover the inside of the plate with a generous layer of glue. Lay your nest-building materials in place. Let dry.

3 Add more glue to the outer edges of the material and let it partially dry. Then add more nest-building material to make a true nest shape.

4 Add a few twigs, sticks, or string to give your nest a more realistic look.

5 Wad and shape pieces of tissue paper into bird eggs. Glue the eggs in place.

More Ideas

We made a bird out of tissue paper and gave it a paper beak and googly eyes. Can you figure out how to make an eagle or duck nest?

Dino and Crab

Paper plates make great bodies for some exotic creatures.

You Will Need:

- flexible dinner-sized paper plates
- scissors
- stapler
- paint, crayons, markers

1 Paint the bottoms of two paper plates for the bodies. Use them whole or cut out sections. Cut out a head and neck, tails, legs, and claws and paint them.

2 Insert these parts between the body plates and staple them rim-to-rim. Decorate with more paint, crayons, or markers and add facial features.

More Ideas

Your creature can "walk" if you use metal fasteners to attach its legs. Can you make an octopus or a spider?

Birds of a Feather

These are birds from a plate. How many different ones can you make?

You Will Need:

- paper plates
- crayons or markers
- scissors
- glue
- stapler
- hole punch
- metal fastener
- yarn

1 Use plates of any size. Draw an outline of a bird's body in the middle of a plate, letting the rim on one side of the plate be the bird's tail and the rim directly opposite it be the bird's beak.

2 Hold a second plate against the first plate bottom-to-bottom. Cut along the outline of the bird you drew. (You'll have two bird bodies.) You'll notice that we even gave our red bird some "feet."

3 Make a set of wings by drawing an outline on a piece of the leftover plate. Hold a second piece against the first back-to-back and cut. You can make several styles of wings like ours.

4 Glue the two bodies together, leaving the tails unglued. Create an eye on each side of the head and attach the wings with glue, staples, or a metal fastener.

5 Find the balance point where your bird will hang as though flying, punch a hole, and string a 20"-24" length of yarn through the hole. Bend the wings away from the bird's body, fluff its tail, and hang your feathered friend where it can "fly."

More Ideas

Color or paint a white plate like a robin to signal the coming of spring, or create eagles to celebrate Independence Day.

Birds like these would look great on the mobile described on page 23.

Ponds and Paths

A paper plate makes a perfect base for all sorts of places. We created a charming duck pond, a wildlife watering hole, an old-fashioned train track, and a scenic bike path.

You Will Need:

- paper plate or platter
- paint, crayons, markers
- poster board
- scissors
- glue or tape
- tissue paper
- old magazines
- bark, sand, rocks, and dried weeds
- yarn

To Make the Base

1 Decide which thing you want your plate to be. The techniques for making the pond, track, bike path, or watering hole will be the same. Only your colors, designs, stand-ups, and materials will differ.

2 Choose any paper plate. Sturdy ones will probably work best. Cut a slit in the plate at each place where you want to put an animal or object. Plan carefully or cut your slits after you make your objects.

To Make the Duck Pond

Color the inside of a paper plate blue to look like water in a pond. Color a section with brown paint mixed with sand around the blue to look like a sandy bank. Color the outer edge green to look like grass. Add gray rocks. Cut out ducks from poster board, leaving a rectangular tab at the bottom. Insert the tabs into the slits you made in the plate. Turn the plate over, fold the tabs, and glue or tape them to the bottom. Add scenery and you've got ducks swimming in a quiet pond.

40

These crafts can be paper sculptures—perfect for centerpieces or desk decorations. Just think of someone you'd like to surprise and make a sculpture of someplace they really like.

To Make the Watering Hole

Color the plate with shades of green, brown, and yellow to look like the ground of the African plain. Use blue for the watering hole. You should have already cut slits where you want to place your animals, bushes, and trees. Draw and cut out African animals or cut some from old magazines as we did. Put a tab on the bottom of each one. Draw and cut out trees and bushes with tabs. Arrange your animals, trees, and bushes on the plate, putting the tabs into the slits and taping them underneath the plate.

To Make the Train Track

Color the plate to look like the "ground." (Gray paint mixed with sand works well.) You can use yarn or markers and crayons to create the tracks. Remember to cut slits where you want your train to be. Draw and cut out a steam engine, cars, and a caboose. Make a tab on the bottom of each one. Put the tabs into the slits and attach them to the plate. We added a station, water tower, and a tree. Have fun creating your own scenery.

To Make the Bike Path

Color the plate to look like the ground of the countryside. We colored a rock wall with gray paint mixed with sand. Add a stream if you like. Draw and color a bike path. Add pictures of trees, bushes, and people on bicycles cut from old magazines—or draw your own on poster board. Put a tab on the bottom of each one. Be sure the slits are where you want your scenery and bikers to be. Put the tabs into the slits and attach them to the plate. We added pieces of bark and dried weeds along the path.

More Ideas

Think of other kinds of tracks you can make. How about horse or car racing? Look in old magazines for pictures of crowds of people and see if you can figure out how to attach a grandstand full of people to the edge of your track.

You can even make a track like the ones on the campus of your local high school. Can you show a stick figure jumping hurdles?

How about creating a frozen pond filled with gliding skaters or a lake full of sail boats?

Hats Galore

Heads are round, hats are round, plates are round. You could go round and round all day making hats. Here are some ideas.

You Will Need:

- dinner-sized paper plates
- paper bowl
- scissors
- poster board
- glue
- paint, crayons, markers
- string or yarn
- ribbon
- button

To Make a Party Hat

Cut a large circle from poster board. Cut it in half and shape one half into a cone. Cut a section of rim from a paper plate to use as the hat's brim. Make notches or tabs along the inner edge of the brim so you can glue it to the cone. Looking at our picture will help you. Create a decoration special to you. We drew and cut out a clown. Glue your decoration to the cone. Add tie-on strings.

You can make small party hats for dolls or to use as party favors by forming a cone from half of a flexible paper plate. Decorate with sparkles and tassels.

To Make the Hat Wall Hanging

Glue a soup bowl upside down in the center of the front of a dinner-sized plate. Paint or color your hat anyway you choose. Can you make it look like straw? Glue ribbon around the area where the plate and bowl are glued together and add decorations. Make a yarn hanger and find a special place to hang your hat.

Make a wall-hanging hat to suit all seasons just by creating different decorations. How about robins for spring, flowers for summer, leaves for fall, and snowflakes for winter?

To Make a Cap

Cut a brim from the center of a paper plate or from a section of the rim. Make tabs where the brim will attach to the cap part. Fold tabs up and glue to the inside of an upside-down paper bowl. Decorate with crayons, paint, or markers. Glue a button to the top.

More Ideas

Make a cap for each of your favorite sports teams. Hang them on the wall of your room.

Or make lots of caps. Write a person's name on each and use them as place cards. This would be a great idea for an end-of-season sports banquet.

Bunny Basket

Create a cuddly dish.

1 Color both sides of 3 plates. Fold 2 of the plates in half. Place one part of each folded plate on top of the third plate. Hold in place with paper clips. Punch holes around the rim, then lace the plates together with yarn. The vertical part of each plate will be the bunny's body.

2 Cut ears from a plate's rim, color, and attach them with metal fasteners. Glue on a nose and a cotton ball for a tail. Add eyes and yarn whiskers. Open the bunny up and stuff with grass and treats.

More Ideas

Instead of ears, add the neck and head of a swan. Or make antlers and a red nose for you-know-who.

Paper-Plate Christmas Tree

Make an ornament.

1 Cut the rim off a paper plate. Cut the rim into sections, going from large to small. The smallest section should have a pointed top.

2 Paint the sections green and glue them in place to form a tree as shown in the picture.

3 Decorate your tree with glitter, sequins, small beads, or cut-paper ornaments.

More Ideas

Create a wintertime mural. Make a forest of trees and decorate with snow made from white paper cutouts.

Amusement Park Plates

You can make a pretend amusement park for your action figures or dolls. We'll give you brief directions for making a few rides. You'll probably think of other park attractions to make.

You Will Need:

- paper plates
- cardboard tubes
- paint, crayons, markers
- hole punch
- poster board
- tape
- glue
- yarn, string
- detergent bottle caps
- wooden dowel
- plastic straws
- chenille sticks

To Make Spinning Swings

1 Decorate both sides of two sturdy dinner-sized paper plates and a cardboard tube. (We used a 7" tube.) Glue the tube to the front side of one of the plates. This will be the swing's top. Punch two holes in the edge of the plate about 1/2" apart. Punch other pairs of holes evenly around the plate's edge.

2 Draw and cut out seats from poster board. Attach them to the top plate with yarn or string. We taped one end of the yarn to the back of the seat, threaded the other end through one of the pairs of holes in the top, and then tied it underneath.

3 Make the swing's bottom by gluing the tube to the middle of the other plate. Finish off your swing with decorative detergent bottle caps on top and bottom.

To Make the Twirling Spaceship Ride

1 Make two flying saucers as described on page 8. We colored ours with crayons and markers. You may choose to paint yours or use colored plates. Find a long cardboard tube and decorate it. We used an 18" wrapping paper tube.

2 Cut a hole the size of the tube in the middle of the bottom layer of each spaceship. Put glue on each end of the tube and stick the tube's ends into the holes. Let the materials dry thoroughly before proceeding.

3 Poke a small hole on each side of the tube halfway between the spaceships. Insert an 18" wooden dowel. You can balance the ends of the dowel on two level surfaces or just hold it and give the spaceships a spin.

To Make a Monster Slide

1 Follow the basic directions for the spiral on page 25. Alter the shape and decorations to suit your design.

2 Decorate a cardboard tube. Glue the bottom of the tube to a poster board circle to help the tube stand more steadily. Attach the top of your spiral to the top of the tube and let it loosely wind around the tube to form the slide.

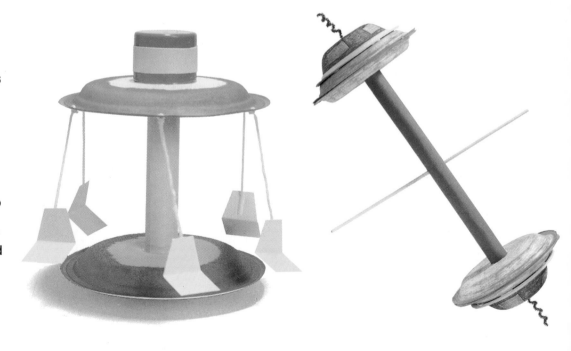

Sometimes boys and girls celebrate birthdays with a group of friends at an amusement park. Wouldn't a craft-making, amusement-park party be fun, too?

To Make the Merry-Go-Round

1 Decorate the bottom of two plates and a cardboard tube cut to 8". Securely attach the tube to the front side of the top plate with glue or tape.

2 Use 4 or 5 straws to make merry-go-round poles that are 8" long. Determine where you want the poles to be, spacing them evenly. Secure the poles to the plates by threading a chenille stick so that it sticks out the ends of the straw. Then bend the chenille sticks to form top and bottom tabs. Tape, glue, or staple the tabs to the top plate.

3 Attach the tube and the straw tabs to the bottom plate with glue, tape, or staples. Glue detergent bottle caps to the top and bottom of the carousel. Cut out or create a picture for each straw pole. Animals or vehicles would work well. Tape the pictures to the straws facing out.

More Ideas

Create some paper dolls or make stick-figure people from chenille sticks. Tape or glue them to the slide, swings, and merry-go-round.

Create a script for a play or movie that takes place in an amusement park. Use these craft creations as props and scenery. Work with some friends and together give an amusing performance.

Balloon Bat

Here's a great make-it, play-it idea.

You Will Need:
- large paper plate
- paint, crayons, markers
- colored glue
- glue
- jumbo craft sticks or tongue depressors
- balloon

1 Decorate a plate with whatever materials you like. We used several shades of colored glue on ours.

2 Glue one stick to the middle of the back of the plate. For a longer handle, glue another stick to the first stick with about a 1" overlap.

3 Blow up a balloon to about softball size and see how many times you can bounce the balloon off the bat.

More Ideas
Make two bats and play pretend tennis with a friend.

Jigsaw Plate

You can make a puzzle for yourself or one to give to a friend who's about to go on a long car trip.

You Will Need:
- sturdy dinner-sized paper plates
- pencil
- markers or crayons
- scissors

1 Decorate your plate. Color a realistic scene or create an abstract design like ours. Carefully cut the plate apart into puzzle-shaped pieces. You might want to lightly sketch outlines of the pieces before you begin cutting.

2 Use a second plate as a base on which to reassemble your puzzle. You may want to draw the shapes of the pieces on the base plate if it is going to be for younger children. Store your puzzle in a plastic bag.

More Ideas
Cut the puzzle pieces into geometric shapes. Or write a message on the puzzle and give it to a secret pal to put together.

Paper-Plate Garden

You can make a flower garden from paper plates. We'll show you three, and you'll probably have some great ideas of your own. Can you think of how you might use layers or sections of paper plates to make a rose or a zinnia?

You Will Need:

- a variety of paper plates
- scissors
- paint, crayons
- chenille sticks
- brown tissue paper
- glue
- construction paper
- pencil
- ruler
- metal fastener

The Folding Flower

Take a flexible paper plate and trim away part of its edges so that the plate is wavy all around. Paint the plate to show a center and petals. Cut slits at intervals all the way around, or try a fringed or jagged cut. (Space between cuts can vary.) Fold and shape segments to look like petals. You could fold some petals up and some back, or try to curl petals with a pencil. Bend a chenille stick to form stem and leaves, then tape it to the back of the flower.

The Sunflower

Paint or color a paper plate or use a bright-yellow colored one. Glue crumpled pieces of brown tissue paper on the plate to make the flower's center. Use cut-out pieces of a paper plate or construction paper to make the stem and leaves. Glue the leaves and stem to the flower.

More Ideas

Instead of making the center of the sunflower, glue on a circular-shaped photo of someone special. Straws, sticks, or tongue depressors can also be used to make stems.

The Blooming Tulip

Mark a pencil point on the edge of a plate. On the opposite side of the plate mark 2 points about 4" apart. Use a ruler to draw two lines, starting at the two points and meeting at the opposite point. Then cut on the lines. You'll have three pieces. Next cut a V in the tip of the cone-shaped piece. Paint the pieces your favorite tulip color or use colored paper plates. Connect the 3 parts of the bloom with a metal fastener as shown below. To make a stem, cut a 1" strip from the center of a paper plate. Use the leftover pieces for leaves and attach to the stem.

Title Index

Subject Index